HORSES

FARM ANIMAL DISCOVERY LIBRARY

Lynn M. Stone

Rourke Corporation, Inc.
Vero Beach, Florida 32964

PHOTO CREDITS

All photos by the author

ACKNOWLEDGEMENTS

The author thanks the following for assistance in the
preparation of photos for this book: Walker Standardbred Farm,
Maple Park, Ill.; Paul Rosenwinkle, Huntley, Ill.; Herb Ruh,
Big Rock, Ill.

LIBRARY OF CONGRESS
Library of Congress Cataloging-in-Publication Data
Stone, Lynn M.
  Horses / by Lynn M. Stone.

    p. cm. — (Farm animal discovery library)
    Summary: An introduction to the physical characteristics,
habits, and natural environment of horses and their relationship
to humans.
    ISBN 0-86593-035-X
    1. Horses—Juvenile literature. [1. Horses.] I. Title. II. Series:
Stone, Lynn M. Farm animal discovery library.
MI302.S76   1990
636.1—dc20   89-29871
                                           CIP
                                           AC

A Foal

TABLE OF CONTENTS

HORSES

Before cars and tractors and trucks, Americans depended upon horses *(Equus caballus)*.

Horses are still found on American farms, but use of the horse has changed.

Unlike other large farm animals, which are raised mostly for their meat, horses are kept largely for pleasure. After all, few farmers need horses. Modern vehicles have seen to that!

Domestic, or tame, horses were first brought to America about 500 years ago by Spanish explorers. Since then, horses have played a major part in American farming, transportation, and war.

Standardbred stallion

HOW HORSES LOOK

Most horses are large and powerful. They have hoofs, long tails and **manes,** and large eyes.

Draft, or work, horses are the biggest. Some of them stand nearly six feet tall from ground to shoulder and weigh more than 2000 pounds.

The average horse is about five feet tall at the shoulders.

Horses may be black, white, a shade of brown, or a mixture of colors.

Draft horses are sturdier than horses that are used for riding. A draft horse has a short, arched neck and deep chest.

Standardbred stallion

WHERE HORSES LIVE

Horses live in a wide variety of conditions. In North America they are found from Mexico north through the United States and Canada. They also live in the cold of Iceland and the heat of Arabia.

The United States has over 10 million horses, second only to China. In the early 1900's, the United States had nearly 20 million horses.

Some horses are kept on farms that have other animals, too. Large numbers of horses are raised on horse farms.

Standardbred horse farm
in Illinois

BREEDS OF HORSES

The first horses to be tamed, or domesticated, were probably wild tarpans. These horses, now **extinct,** lived in Europe.

From the early domestic horses, horses of different sizes, shapes, and colors were developed. Each separate group of horses became known as a **breed.**

Today there are well over 100 different breeds of horses.

The thoroughbred and standardbred, for example, are racing horses. The quarter horse is a favorite of cowboys. The 2000-pound Belgian is a strong, gentle draft horse.

Icelandic pony
in Iceland

Thoroughbred horses

Belgian mare

WILD HORSES

The first horses in North America were the size of dogs. They lived some 50 million years ago.

As time passed, horses became larger.

These horses vanished from North America long ago. The so-called wild horses in North America now are relatives of domestic horses that escaped from farms.

The wild horses called mustangs live in the dry, open country of the West.

Truly wild horses are the Przewalski's horse, onager, and kiang of Asia. The African wild ass and zebras are also wild horses. They live in Africa.

Wild Przewalski horse

BABY HORSES

Baby horses are called **foals.** Foals stand on their long, wobbly legs soon after they are born. Within just a few hours they can run short distances.

By its first birthday, a horse is about half-grown. Young male horses are known as **colts.** Females are called **fillies.**

A horse reaches full size by its fifth birthday. Fully-grown female horses are **mares.** Male horses which can father foals are **stallions.**

Horses often live to be from 20 to 30 years old.

*Standardbred
mare and foal*

HOW HORSES ARE RAISED

In warm weather, horses graze in pastures or fenced areas called **paddocks.** Horses are also fed grain and hay.

A horse's home in the barn is called a stall. Each stall is walled so that the horses are separated from each other.

Horses are often brushed and combed in their stalls. Horse care may include having flat, metal rings—horseshoes—put on the horse's hooves. Horseshoes help protect the feet of horses which walk or gallop on hard surfaces.

*Quarter horses
and thoroughbreds*

HOW HORSES ACT

Horses are fairly intelligent animals. They have good memories, and they learn to respond to many commands.

Horses tend to be nervous. Even a shadow can "spook" a horse, making it run in panic.

Owners of draft horses outfit them with blinders. Blinders attach to the leather straps on a horse's head. Blinders reduce the horse's vision on each side.

Stallions are very powerful and excitable animals. Stallions are far more likely to kick or bite than a mare.

Belgian draft horses

HOW HORSES ARE USED

The number of horses in the United States now is about half of what it was in 1910.

In the early part of the 20th century, cars and the "iron horse"—the train—moved horses aside.

Horses are still popular for sports such as polo and racing. A horse can run a mile in about one and one-half minutes. Horses are also used for pleasure riding.

On a few farms, horses are used to pull wagons or plow.

Glossary

breed (BREED)—closely related group of animals that came about through man's help; a type of domestic horse

colt (COLT)—young male horse

domestic (dum ES tik)—tamed and raised by man

draft (DRAFT)—refers to an animal that works for man, especially one which pulls

extinct (ex TINKT)—completely gone, disappeared forever

filly (FILL ee)—young female horse

foal (FOAL)—a baby horse

mane (MANE)—the long hair that rises along a horse's neck from forehead to shoulders

mare (MAER)—an adult female horse

paddock (PAD ik)—a fairly small, fenced area outdoors for horses

stallion (STAL yun)—an adult male horse

INDEX